A Fantasy BOOK of Poetry and Stories representing some of the authors thoughts

& challenges inspired by his take on his journey through life thus far & bearing in m

ind the limit of his understanding of the workings of things from personal research

and life experiences as surreal and as wacky as they might appear.

This book serves as a reference

material for the author to inspire and continue to be inspired.

The journey of
a thousand miles
begins with one step

I. Life and it's Meaning

The greatest puzzle that has baffled me the most is the meaning of "الم" (Alif lam

mim) ,for the sake of the reader to gain perspective and insight into my world I

will consider my use of the likeness of the words in bracket to mean

"Source" or " Prime Matter".

Alas it's been approximately about 2 years in, I feel a little more of this thing embedded in me called feeling (fee-ling). (Cry-eat-sleep-poop-chuckle-play) seems to be the most efficient codes for this program (thoughts running through my mind)(things in head) it comes with the package the body I hear some people say (investigate!).

These beings I see & hear everyday in all shapes and sizes, they seem somewhat similar to me (c-e-s-p-c-p) but I don't really see them poop (invstg8). Hmm interesting!

So what to do what to do, getting tired of these diapers I might as well look deeper into these shapes and words so I can communicate with these weird adult beings.

I see father only that much, rarely like never, but I miss father, I hear he is going through depression etc., he sure looks happy when I see him, I sure hope he is not depressed because of me hmm (IV8).

Lesson learned:

Adult man seems to like to label and categorize everything. I need to be watchful around these old folks. I would use Play as my prime decoy to Investigate em.

Hmm. I'm loving this new life already! Its INTERESTING!

2. Essence and Worldly Worlds

33 years in and finally getting comfortable, the journey has been a long one, full of treachery and love, gotta love it. But uno what they say " life is still a bitch" LOL.

So now that understanding has been upgraded back to a time of shapes there seems to be no more need for words or is there?

Mind body soul or is it body soul essence or is it body and essence. U see my dilemma, just so I don't loose my way utterly I would stick to 1 2 3, seems basic enough I assume.

I never stop asking WHY! Even for Telepathy I say WHY! Why me! Why Now! Why Ever! I literarily want no part of this. I feel as though my hand was forced, I laid my bed and so I had to sleep on it at some point. My inquisitiveness gave rise to my found understanding in some matters and wisdom in some others.

Lord Buddha, I must say gave me the most strength when I needed it the most.

Thank you Buddha Spirit, Thank you for reminding me to have fun with this experience cos after all its only an experience that came to you divinitively.

I thank you but please give me the heads up next time, cos this shit is DEEP!

Aaa MI TUO FO

3. yin yang $ Lao Tsu

So looking into ancient Asian philosophy, delving deep into ancient cultures trying to gain some understanding seeking seeking cos therein seems wisdom of the ages.

Embedded within source prime. I see a world looking inwards in myself gaining understanding thinking in alignment trying to align with a school of thought but alas we same as ya'll tryna figure this shit out aswell. After searching and searching I begin to see a pattern emanating from within self, some mixture of material fusion to create a sense of well being safety in alignment towards the very goal of seekers and sages. Understanding bequeath on me shows a fusion between entities to create source prime alas more understanding shows fusion not dissolution. (inv8).

Lesson learned:

find balance, embrace your demons shine brighter with your light!

Lao Tsu

Great man great thinker astrologer believer from limited sources I see a pattern towards the union of opposites antonyms from poems that bestow some perspective but my link power is limited, my level of understanding shallow in comparison to the depth of depths the deepest of the deepest. I see wisdom beyond comparison. Words elude me!

Lesson learned:

Wisdom is bestowed to a few understanding to many.

4. The alchemist of old

Kimiya-yi sa'ādat (The Alchemy of Happiness) – a text on Islamic philosophy and spiritual alchemy by Al-Ghazālī (1058-1111).
https://en.wikipedia.org/wiki/Kimiya-yi_sa'ādat

Now what do we have here: interesting interesting interesting to what end seeking

I see secrets great secrets kept away from common man but loose its way always comes and knocks on the door when he already inside pressing your buttons.

Transforming, transmuting materials shaping entities to create price oh not price again don't get me started.

But price is already off the table at this point cos some shit don't got no price.

So looking closer seeking seeking I see balance union synchronicity the music of the universe of the multiverses beyond beyond.

Lesson learned:

The moon and the sun: Oceanic & Magnetic currents : Micro-Phyto-Benthos: All life matters

5. Alexander and Cleopatra

More war and love and more war history cultures rituals fighting loving fighting and more loving. Hmm Interesting! Rich! If all is not everything then all is nothing!

I see wisdom I see Egypt!!Hopeful!!

The truth is we could write more books on history and we would still not be able to source the most accurate information about Alex and Cleo, I tell you this though: them guys were wise beyond their years believe it or not, they were greater than great, greater than Buffet or Zuck in todays world if you catch my drift, richer than rich in both knowledge and riches so I plead no contest. I however, came across a passage that I tag to Cleo understanding that the pursuit of that ultimate alchemical concoction could never be complete without it containing all of life all prime matter. So, you get me now, I really do plead no contest and reserve my right to! LOL. I know I chickened out of that one. But eh, what say you dear reader?

6. Egypt land of Ra

Nuff said! Speechless! Speechless! Godly!

The eye of Ra the lonely lioness!

Tears of the Sun! Nuff Said! 'Limitless Scorpion Sub-zero Akuma //Kratos// Goku and Vegeta Blanka' dreaming Godly dreams.

Is possible even possible? Questions more Questions??

Lessons Learned:

Impossible is possible, so "Under the Sun anything is possible".

"Change is the only constant thing in Life Accompanied by death as a watcher"

7. Economic warfront

Civilization>Interesting: lets try this out maybe just maybe it might just

WORK/./<IV8>

Power: Control of decisions that effect/affect change observable/unobservable change.

Power and Politics. Hmm. Interesting!

Time has to mediate!!! Dear or Dear Time You being all mighty and all and the sole exchange for life you have to stay and keep watch while the sons and daughters of Adam and the Jinn's and the Animalia are somewhat forgetful (Amnesiac) we wish only a peak back at what you see oh dear time seer of seers.

Okay man oh man you being the mediary <likeness intermediary> of worlds produce to me something of such marvel that shows your appreciation for me OH Time!

And he produced such a marvel as to keep watch of time without life source as its battery birth date 1884 before the official birth of the great order of 1888.

Ye man produced a Breitling%<> wrist watch to Inspire greatness and yet again price lurked its head.

Ye Man lacked wisdom and therein he learned a big lesson!!!

8. The Mundane

ZOMBIES AND ROBOTS BEFRIENDING DEMONS AND ANGELS

Its really all falling apart by now if you catch my drift but no! Shinigami tells a different tale! IV8!

9.Adam and the question why?

Mother/IV8/Father But WHY!IV8*888*

Lesson Learned:

Make your own Instruction manual, there's way to many of ya"ll to download to Simultaneously especially since ya"ll been making more Babies I hear

"Babies making Babies"

Ya"ll Just Seek it and in Time you shall Find

Time: Enough time for time to pass over time and still be enough time to do it again

10. Instant Parallel universes; "With immediate Alacrity"

"It has to be true, where else do we find hope in the land full of hope"

So if Life can exist instantaneously on different plains, my question is how many of these plains should ye man be privy to, considering the limitations of his body and brainpower to actually comprehend and absorb the realities, or to at least be able to make flight or fight instinctive decisions about.

For my own sanity I choose 1,2,3 plains, seems plausible and comprehensible enough, I predict though anymore than 3 plains, madness would instinctively start to play old tricks just like its cousin loose its way.

II. The black hole

"DON'T GET SUCKED IN"

"The Deeper the hole the louder the Noise"

It is all in mans power to control the limit of his madness, by limiting your absorption of knowledge, you limit your level of understanding and by ye Gods I pray to only be granted such understanding as I may withstand and function properly in the mundane world, because anymore and wisdom beckons.

12. The number 8

Is Life a Game of Chance, Chess or is Serendipity real???

"Oje ko je"

Roots mould you nourishes you fills you motivates you inspires you and in the end what say you?

At the end of your story what would have been your contribution to we oh mother/lfather.

"Life will be your price now roll your dice"

13. An Alternative approach to battle Some mental health issues:

(the 6 demons!)

"Insomnia: lack of sleep or sleep deprivation"

Patient Story: I longed for sleep but sleep hid from me, I thought we had made peace I thought the alliances made were solid but yes they were solid you just needed to switch up so we switched you up on this end but you did not show understanding enough to feel the message.

Lesson learned:

Do what you do to show appreciation to Time the Keeper of secrets when sleep hides from you. Seek tiredness if you must!

Soak in the Time!

Anxiety: "Nervous Surge of Energy or lack of!"

Patient Story: Crowds, 1 2 3 and it already starts feeling too much,

Thoughts running round and round, I feel them, all around me. Need to get away

NOW!

But no its all in my head!

MAINTAIN FOCUS RELAX DEEP BREATHES STEP BACK OF THE MOMENT

(−1−2−3)!!!

And Action!

(1 2 3)!!!

Breath Deepens Sweating Dries up You feel Cool Calm and Collected

and

You Connect!!!

Instanta!!!

Life grants you a glimpse into greatness you see it but cannot even feel it your glimpse fades into the horizon. Noted!!

And you claimed you were ready. Sons and Daughters of Adam!

Lesson learned:

TRY TO KEEP YOUR COOL even when all is lost because change has made an eternal promise to keep things moving, backed by alliances from beyond beyond!

Seasons Change so be watchful and seize your moment!

"Depression: Sadness"

Patient Story: It should pass I hear, they say just do this, take that and just do that and it will pass I hear. Hear from who?<IV8>*

Have they been through it? I mean what I'm going through? Or tell me at least something similar? Oh they read it! Did they understand it? Oh they treated others! Not sure but we are sure they are just trying to help.

<<IV8>*=NULL>

Lesson learned:

Let sadness also have its time it also pays its price!!!Happiness.

<u>Psychosis: abnormal<1V8>/ /thoughts<1V8></u>

Patient Story: Oh man Guy you are nearing the deep end I hear the deeper the hole the louder the noise. But what if I'm not after noise and I'm not after anything in particular what then?

Oh man you are OYO with that one

What you mean OYO, I mean OYO= On your own <LOL>

Have they been through it? I mean what I'm going through? Or tell me at least something similar? Oh they read it! Did they understand it? Oh they treated others! Not sure but we are sure they are just trying to help.

However bossman we hear you been on the ganja thing as of late what say ye?

YES I DID IT. I smoked some ganja and it felt NICE! It gave me an ethereal world I could find some solace in for when I needed it! Though it increased the paranoia and psychosis but I found out that there was always the defective gene we never really examined thoroughly. So at this point I'm not really sure where to go for more knowledge to seek understanding for life to bequeath on me wisdom on this topic.

Though You had a chance to ask them if they think the mind and body are connected and what say ye?

NUFF SAID!

Class in progress!!!

" Paranoia: Fear"

Hmm. Been hearing about this defective gene theory not sure what it means but seems to me that it could be evolutions back up plan.

Satiation = 8

More Knowledge is needed = 8

Solace may be required but not necessary, connections are needed for more knowledge!!!

"Addiction: is characterized by compulsive engagement in stimuli, despite

adverse consequences

So let me get this straight addiction was one of the ORIGINAL keepers

the watchers, are you saying addiction is ********!

WORDS ELUDE ME!!!

MORE KNOWLEDGE IS NEEDED FOR MORE UNDERSTANDING SO THAT

LIFE MAY BEQUEATH ON ME WISDOM OF THE AGES!!!

<u>THE AUTHOR</u>

My inspiration has been climaxed by the realization of the synchronicity that exists between all life material and ethereal love playing its role interweaving itself within everything in existence while sadness lurks around the corner accompanied by death forming alliances with watchers and keepers of time.

I was born in Lagos Nigeria on the 23rd day of November 1983AD to the AGBOLUAJES of Okefoko OYO State Kinsmen of the tribe of YORUBA formerly known as YaRBA descendants of SANGO the GOD of thunder and kinsmen of Kings and Kinship recorded history retrievable as far back as 1753AD.

I now reside in Toronto Ontario, a nationalized Canadian a proud dad and a proud WorldSage!!!.

Lesson learned thus far:

At this point you should realize the role that words play in fashioning out futures of futures, be wise in your actions keep them sustainable find balance achieve union with your energy source your life source

your Qi.

Found massive Inspiration from the below Figure depicting the Golden Rule sourced freely from the internet on November 17 2016 AD